SRS BOOKS

Books available by myself under various names such as Sarah Ruth Scott and Simon Robert Sinclair

EIGHT SKULLS OF TEVERSHAM

CRACKED PORCELAIN

FOR THE LOVE OF CHARLOTTE

STORIES BEYOND BELIEF 1 and 2

CURSED

BLOOD TRAIL – ACROSS TIME

CONFLICT OF FAITH

UNDERSTANDING JODIE

OPERATION BRAINSTORM

DOUBLE EXPOSURE

CRACKED PORCELAIN –ACTS OF ABUSE

To Malcolm Best Regards Steve Sutton

Deep
in
Thought

MORE POEMS FROM THE JAR

STEPHEN SUTTON

authorHOUSE®

AuthorHouse™ UK
1663 Liberty Drive
Bloomington, IN 47403 USA
www.authorhouse.co.uk
Phone: 0800 047 8203 (Domestic TFN)
        +44 1908 723714 (International)

Published by AuthorHouse 12/28/2019

ISBN: 978-1-7283-9724-5 (sc)
ISBN: 978-1-7283-9723-8 (e)

Acknowledgements

Thank you to my son Daniel Robert Sutton for agreeing to be on the front cover of the book, it is usually my daughter Jennifer May Sutton or friends such as Kari Cooper and Bethany Jade Carter. I would like to say many thanks to all my friends at Hawksyard priory nursing home who supported me in my venture, knowing about my disability of dyslexia and dyspraxia. Thank you to my Mother and father Rita and Leonard Sutton who also supported me through the rough times and who believed in me. Thank you Richard William Howarth for being my best friend being there for me as a true friend does. Thank you Mick Morris for doing the same going that extra mile and helping me find my direction. Thanks to Joy Sage and Liz Winfield amongst others who supported me as I did them over the years. Thank you to Carol Aston who has been a long term friend and work colleague at Nearfield house and Hawksyard and will always be in my heart. Thank you to my family who will always be with me Gemma Sutton, Jennifer Sutton, Michael Sutton and Daniel Sutton. Thanks to my aunty Penny who understood my dilemma with dealing with dyslexia and dyspraxia and taught me many things in life. Thank you to my brothers Jim and Andrew Sutton for being there for me helping me to cope with this world and stand up for myself against all odds, which is partly why I am here to tell my story today.

Contents

Acknowledgements..v

Endurance.. 1

Rose 2

Sea Waves... 3

Blank Canvas 4

Tree.. 5

Images of David Bowie 7

John Lennon The Legend.. 8

Legends... 9

Action Hero 10

New York City 11

Gifted 13

Shadows 14

Pride 15

Cracked Porcelain 16

Cracked Porcelain 17

Plastic Dolls And Action Men (From Cracked
Porcelain) 18

Raven (From Cracked Porcelain) 20

Killer Queen 21

Monster... 23

Nightmares 24

Faded Light.. 25

Equality And Diversity... 26

Dyspraxia... 27

Being Different 28

Deep in Thought... 29

Life In A Jar 30

Cursed 31

Witches 32

Eight Skulls Of Teversham............................... 33

Sienna The Vampire Blood Trail-Across Time 34

Just Like Magic 35

Outside The Jar 36

School Daze 38

Scars... 39

Father... 41

Calm Waters 43

Shield My Love 44

Prisoner 45

Operation Brainstorm 46

The Inner Truth 47

Loves Hope 49

Emily In Ecstacy Once More 50

Then Came The Rain... 52

Ancient Ruins 53

Let The Candles Burn 55

The Stone Bridge By The Stream 56

Soldier.. 57

Nothing is Real... 58

All or Nothing 59

The Vision... 60

Time 61

Sea Waves... 62

The Journey... 63

Scotland 64

My Best Friend..65

About The Author 67

Endurance

Do your best in all you do
And do it well, it's up to you
You can be anything that you want to be
Just make the effort and you will see

Take all the steps and deal with the hate
Climb up the ladder and open the gate
No matter what your disability may be
You will endure it, just wait and see

Be ever positive and what you've got
In order to achieve this you will receive a lot
With years of endurance pain and endeavour
You will have a life of fun and absolute pleasure

Rose

I watch you bloom into a flower
And laze away a midday hour
You seem to blossom right before my eyes
It was there and then I realise
That life is passing how very wise

You open all your petals in the sun
I know from this that life's just begun
I smell the fragrance of your bud
And life goes on as if it should

Throughout the summer warm and bright
You are a wonder a glorious sight
The days go by in their formation
And you remain in your location

The wind and rain comes in force
Thrashing about without remorse
But you remain without surrender
My budding rose in all your splendour

Sea Waves

The waves roll along a beach
Sparking under the sun
By the morn I see
That the day has just begun

Gently it flows across the sand
As clear as can be
With a faint whisper of a sound
All for us to see

So peaceful and flowing
It glides over the sand
Like the beat of my heart
Or the wave of my hand

Away from the chaos
The noise on the street
With the sea waves
Around my bare feet

Sea waves on the ocean
Sea waves on the sand
Moving to music and
The wave of my hand

Blank Canvas

Blank canvas waiting for me
I wonder what the artist can see
A person an object something to do
I want to create a painting for you

Splashes of white, swirls of green
The best image that you've ever seen
All from my thought from my weird mind
All known images things of this kind

Colours have meaning like the words of a book
Just search around you please take a look
Like word from a poet on blank paper you know
Follow my guidance just have a go

Painting by mood colours so dark
Dim is your vision you left your mark
Painting so bright show your display
This is his best work I hear them say

The blank canvas begins a journey you see
A fine creation for you and me
Thinking of colours I think of red
Now it is completed its time for bed

Tree

How I wish that I were a tree
With lot's of people admiring me
With lots of branches and leave to see
All adorned in my majesty

How I wish I were a tree
With the wind blowing through me
Waving about what a spectacle to see

How I wish I was a tree
What a sight I could be
Standing there for all to see
And no one to answer to just totally free

How I wish I were a tree
How profound that would be
Branches reaching to the sky
Dropping leave on those passing by
And the fruits that I bear
Falling apples everywhere
Or chestnuts dropping on the ground
Isn't it funny and so profound?
Oh how happy I would be if was only a living tree

Images of David Bowie

On with the make up and glitter too
Bowie is made up to entertain you
With Ziggy standing on the stage
Like a performer from another age

With his spiky long hair on show
And glittery suit he's ready to go
Singing songs of time and space
With make up on his face

His voice gives a distinctive sound
And helps to provide joy all around
Glam rock is a thing of this day
As the seventies gets under way

By the eighties Bowie changes his style
Although he carries a distinctive smile
His stage presence is one to admire
The suits are part of his attire
He writes the songs and plays the tune
Flies through space up to the moon
Surviving bad times with his life in tact
Bowie is a legend and that is a fact

John Lennon The Legend

A man that was meant to be
A raw voice singing energy
Spilling out such melody
Like the man you were meant to be

Singing of love and romance
While you cry out peace rants
People listening when you talk
And many follow you when you walk

Your songs have such meaningful words to me
Speaking of oppression and when we are free
His hate and his anger of war in his day
Could only reflect on others this way

Rock and roll hero
A legend to me
A working class hero
Is something to be

All of his mind games imagine them today
Winston O'Boogie
Is a legend today

Legends

Legends are actors
Part of the screen
Legends are rock stars
Part of the scene

Legends can be ancient
Part of history
Legends are men and women
Read it and see

Legends are made
From the talent they posses
Legends are from greatness
The fruit of success

Being part of a legend
Is part of the game
Being successful
Remember their name

Its about gifts and talent
That you present at the door
People love what you do
And ask for an encore

Action Hero

I want to be an action hero
So I can stop kids bullying me
Brave like an action hero
And walk around totally free

In my dreams I am an action hero
Fighting my way through school
Walking around like an action hero
Instead of somebody's fool

I want to be an action hero
Playing in the school yard
Fighting off all the bullies
Making out to be hard

My life in school at present
Is being pushed against the wall
But my life as an action hero
I have the power to conquer all

New York City

The statue of liberty stands so fine
The lady of the city is so divine
A gift from the French years ago
Here on an island right here on show

In central park we walk along
A busker stands singing a song
With street performers working away
They come along to brighten your day

Artists and singers perform to the crowd
Comics will have you laughing out loud
With tricks to astound you beyond believe
Lennon's memorial has you stricken with grief

Many performers you see at time square
Dressed in costumes just for a dare
Shows are on Broadway only the best
More fine performers on with the show
Prepared for their audience ready to go

Brooklyn is another island close by
With a shopping mall to try
Then theres long island a place to be
Living your life happy and free

New York is a city that stands on its own
With crowded streets and a life in the zone
With cars and buses noise on the street
People pass by us being discrete

Now at ground zero an Éire sight
The bodies of many lost in fright
One time trade centres stood in this place
Now they are fountains a memorial with grace

New York is known for its many stores
Like Macy's for clothes which you see on your tours
With toy shops and Apple stores this kind of thing
Some places sell jewellery plenty of bling

Gifted

You may have talent you may have fame
People may know you and remember your name
People are gifted in some special way
By talking to other and having your say

They may be artistic painting so clear
Or drawing a portrait of someone quite near
Or by making crafts that are put on display
Selling their products or giving them away

True gifts are a treasure and fine they may be
Showing your talent for all to see
On television and in galleries on the internet
Or on You tube they say is the best

People with dyslexia are gifted you say
I am dyslexic so what can I say
Dyspraxics are gifted I heard it is so
I am dyspraxic so what do I know

Watch and observe is this so?
Have I a gift I wouldn't know
If you would like
You let me know

Shadows

Shadows follow me everywhere
I turn around and there is one of them there
Shadows attached to my body so well
They linger round me like a bad smell

Shadows are big and shadows are small
You never can tell where they may fall
They follow you here they follow you there
They won't desert you so never despair

Shadows are seen on pavement or walls
From the shining of light the shadow falls
Dark as the night it will come again soon
By the night light or the light of the moon

Pride

Lift you head up
Be proud of who you are
Be pleased that
You have got this far

Feel comfortable in your body
And your sexuality
Don't be ashamed
Of whom you are meant to be

Speak out and lets
Here you say
I am me I am free
And I am gay

I respect you for
Who you are
You're my child
A rising star

Whatever you are
I am on your side
Walk down these streets
With pride

Cracked Porcelain

THE CRACKED PORCELAIN SAGA

This is a collection of poems from the cracked porcelain saga, some of the best stories from the series developed into poems. It is basically about the life of a psychiatric nurse called Ruth Ashley struggling to survive in a hostile world. Ruth is a lesbian with a history of mental and physical abuse coming to terms with her sexuality and haunted by her past.

Cracked Porcelain

(from the story of the same name)

You were just like porcelain to me
With smooth skin perfect as can be
I kept you clean and free from flaws
Like my ornaments I kept you indoors
The image that I had of you
Was perfection and love that grew

But then my porcelain mask had gone
The colourful image that once shone
Defiled by others with a shameless grin
You had become cracked porcelain

Once you had been a model child
Now you are just crazy and wild
I nurtured a victim of child abuse
Now I could never let my daughter loose

The world turned its back on your beautiful face
Leaving you in such a disgrace
Defiled by others with a shameless grin
Now I know your cracked porcelain

Plastic Dolls And Action Men (From Cracked Porcelain)

From a child I have loved you
And all the time you did not know
We laughed and played as children
Until I had to go

We played with plastic doll and action men
For hours and hours each day
Running round the play room
Till one of us would say

Its time to go it is so late
We left the play room in a state
We seemed to get on so good
Just the way children should

But as we grew my love did grow
Perhaps my feeling then would show
My heart became as heavy as can be
Then he left to join the army

Such a brave man he came to be
He fought for his country and all could see
The man was a hero one of the best
With an array of medals on his chest

He died in battle or so I believe
At this time I was sure to conceive
I had a girl to my surprise
And when I looked she had his eyes

This child was born she was Ken's indeed
One beautiful girl from a perfect seed
But I could not keep her it was the wrong thing to do
So I decided to give her to you

Raven (From Cracked Porcelain)

Beware, beware the ravens claw
Will stab you in the heart
Her dark and sullen image
Will scare you from the start

Raven reveals her madness
And sets about her prey
Leaves her mark upon her victims
She chooses them each day

Beware the evil raven
As she pursues her prey
The dark mysterious raven
With nothing much to say

The raven has a lust for blood
As she goes in for the kill
But she never drinks the blood
She just lets it spill

The raven walks around
With madness in her mind
Anyone she wants to kill
She will seek and find

Killer Queen
(from cracked porcelain)

I want to be like you
With long hair and eyes of blue
Though sometime your wear a frown
I just realised your eyes are brown

I admire your courage
And you are so free
How I wish I were you
Instead of me

I dress like you
Although I am a man
I walk like a woman
And I do what I can

I would kill for you
And protect your name
I am serious you see
This isn't a game

The people who die
Deserve all they get
I do it for you
To pay a great dept
I follow you
As you go out at night
And stay close by you
Keeping you in my sight

You were a victim
Of abuse in the past
They will not harm you
I will get them at last

I changed my body
To look like you
So many changes
I could be you

Monster
(from cracked porcelain)

It's his evil game of treachery
That gives him a name that's meant to be
So cruel and wicked is his name
Or monster which means the same

He lives his life without a friend
And his name with follow unto his end
But this isn't who he is meant to be
He makes peoples lives a misery

The abuse he gives is very wrong
And he will be caught before too long
The abuser deceives his victims you see
By abusing them so mentally

The monster deceives you in everyway
He tries to befriend you within a day
Now he locked within a cell
It's time for him to live in hell

For he lives his life without a friend
And evil stays with him until his end

Nightmares
(from cracked porcelain)

I go to sleep at night
And wake up with a fright
These night terrors keep me awake
Get rid of them for goodness sake

Dream after dream I nod off for a spell
And when I awake I wake up in hell
I find myself wrestling in mood
And hurt myself I am covered in blood

The agony and pain I put myself through
Aren't glad it's me and not you
Night after night I have the same dream
And very often I wake up and scream

Faded Light

Like a faded light
You appeared to me
With a boastful grin
Fading into iniquity

But your sins will get you
In the end
Like meeting
A long lost friend

Like a fading light
You came to be
A subject for
Controversy

This fading light
Is going out
And provide such answers
For those in doubt

Your religion
Will never save the day
Your thoughts will
Just simply fade away

Equality And Diversity

No matter what religion
You profess to be
Think of equality
And diversity

Treating each other
As they want to be
Is equality
And diversity

Each person is
Their own identity
From is you
And freedom is me

Race and gender
Is nobody's choice
You're born this way
So you must rejoice

No one should judge you
For the colour of your skin
Nor the sex that you are
Under that skin

Just because of the difference
You see
No one should mock you
Just let you be

Dyspraxia
(It's just the way I am)

I make such excuse for the way I perform
But I have been like this since I was born
With no sense of direction or lack of control
Or not achieving or reaching my goal

I correct my steps so I don't fall
People laugh and make me small
I cannot even catch a ball
And when I walk I am sure to fall

Some days are good some days I am bad
Sometimes I will curse sometimes I am glad
My brain tells me one thing my body says another
Why am I like this I must ask my mother

Which is my left hand, which is my right?
Should I go to school and end up in a fight?
My routine tends to vary according to my day
Should I concentrate no way I play
It just the way I am I tell myself
I wish I was an ornament sat on a shelf
Something to admire attractive and nice
But this is me with the luck of the dice

Being Different

Walking and talking in your own style
Just being you and wearing a smile
Wearing the clothes that you want to wear
Living your life without a care

Just being different showing your worth
The only one of your kind walking this earth
Alone or with company you're not really fussed
Doing what you want that is a must

Just being different to those you're around
Just being there without making a sound
People love you or hate or find you strange
Or they accept you for you'll never change

Deep in Thought

DEEP IN THOUGHT

By the expression on your face
Your mind is in another place
A place that is distant like the stars
For all I know it could be Mars

In the deepest cavities of your mind
Who will know what you will find
The deepest thoughts, hope and schemes
Solving puzzles or analyzing dreams

Searching for answers of mysteries today
Holding onto thoughts or visions this day
Even more riddles enter your head
That seem accumulate when your in your bed

Life In A Jar

This is a prison of life's long pain
As for the meaning let me explain
People suffer from anxiety and fame
Some are blind, deaf and some are lame
Without all these things they would go very far
Until this time they must live in a jar

Fame restricts you from the freedom to move
Make plans for the future that they disapprove
A clear direct guided by fools around
Controlled like a robot without any sound
You live every day in a jar
A lost identity you don't know who you are

The title is ambiguous as you can see
But it expresses all things to me
Whether you are ill or just a star
Just remember you live in a jar
Who said your world is an oyster expressions like that
Must have been crazy or some sort of Pratt

Cursed

Spirits of the past do see
A curse on a family
Mirrors just to see through
Like a gateway they come for you

Snakes, spiders and creatures come
To menace you when the curse begun
Voices crying out in fear
Touching you when they are near

Swamps devour you when you wake
Waters drown you in a lake
Fire consumes you in this hour
Or poison to your lips so sour

Deadly is the curse at night
You wake up screaming with a fright
Who knows what terror lies within?
As the mirror reveals its mighty Sin

Witches

Witches fly high in the air
Witches dance without a care
They cast their spells late at night
And dance around under the moonlight

Witches cauldrons bubbling with the fire
They dance around and never tire
With cackling sounds they make a fright
Like owls that hoot throughout the night

Witches display magic at night
What a display, an awesome sight
Trick after trick, spell after spell
An incredible sight didn't they do well

Dark witches are legends white witches too
Showing the world all they can do
Halloween is the night for them
They can keep appearing again and again

Eight Skulls Of Teversham

This is a tale of witches or a legend to me
Told of a family from Teversham you see
The horrors and evil which I will unfold
Of murderous dark witches the story is told

The night when the witches evil did slay
Their wicked magic struck on their prey
Eight witches came forth into the night
Killed a young family who couldn't fight

A young boy called Eric swore revenge to them all
By forming an army and the witches would fall
Eight skulls was his trophy to hand to the mayor
Proof of their deaths that he must now share

Death to dark witches and descendants too
Eight more skulls he collected before he was through
But eight had a meaning that the witches new well
It means resurrection as part of a spell
So the witches linger in a cave far away
In a place in Scotland that where they will stay

Sienna The Vampire Blood Trail-Across Time

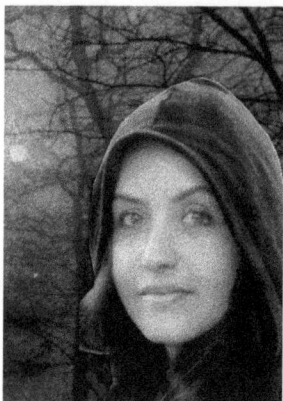

Running through a forest fearful of her life
Sheltered by the trees at night in a dreadful strife
The vampire is alone hunted like a dear
Running through the clearing
There she shall appear

Sheltered in a castle in a darkened room
There she finds a picture in which she is consumed
She falls out of the picture and lands upon a floor
Falls upon an observer close beside a door

This begins her story this is what's foretold
From out of a time portal in this time is told
A vampire from another age desperately seeking a friend
But what is her destiny what is written in the end

Just Like Magic

JUST LIKE MAGIC

It all began in Chantelle's play room one day
She heard the voice of a child as she began to play
Alicia called out from her world
It was a call for help
Chantelle's reaction was very clear
She let out a cry like a yelp

She entered a mirror into her world
Not knowing what I would find
To my surprise this other world
Had put me in a bind

A magic world, a fantasy world
Such a different place
With unicorns and witches
Amongst a different race

Outside The Jar

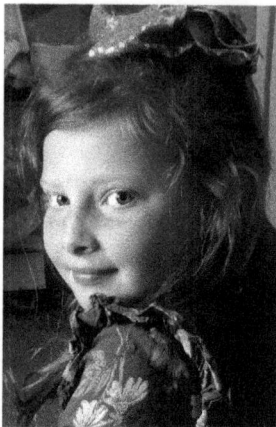

OUTSIDE THE JAR

Life in a jar was a protective zone
Where I lived my life all alone
With dyslexia and asthma keeping me company
Dealing with those now sets me free

Outside to jar is where I dwell
Having left a living hell
The jar was my prisoner I have to tell
From early life was there I fell

I learned to read and write myself
By choosing comics off a shelf
I discovered it was my place to be
By learning a new strategy

The asthma was caused by childhood stress
I could certainly see I was in a mess
I needed to change my state of mind
And leave my painful past behind

I struggled to be who I wanted to be
And now I live in ecstasy
Through education I excelled and now I feel so overwhelmed

School Daze

Those days of being at school
Showing the teacher I am no fool
Sat at a desk staring into space
Not being attentive and you could tell by my face

I wasn't listening my concentration was poor
All I wanted was to leave via the door
Art class was fun I could show off my talent and skill
I had a purpose, a role to forfill

Maths was my weakness fractions a chore
The teachers got frustrated they knew the score
I enjoyed English especially poetry
I enjoyed reciting verse it was fun for me

I liked history and French too
Domestic science and all that baloo
I hated being punished it was such a disgrace
Being hit with a ruler or slapped on my face

Scars

Be who you want to be
Do what you want to do
Live how you want to live
It's up to you

Forget what you need to forget
It's all in the past
Live for the present
It's with you at last

The scars do remind you
Of your past life that has been
Some scars are hidden
They will never be seen

Plan for your future
trips far ahead
But don't dream about them
You can't reach them from your bed

FATHER (Leonard James Sutton) DIED 1993

Father

My mind goes drifting
Back in time I see
The man that
You used to be

When you bounced me
On your knee
Showed me the things
That I needed to see

You guide and taught me
The right way
And gave me the words
That I needed to say

My memories of you
Holidays near the sea
Camping in the field
That was life the for me

Now I miss you
For you have gone
The light in my heart
That has shone
Is dim and fades away
But it relights
At the end of the day

It glows in Heaven
Right up in the sky
And remains there
Until I die

Calm Waters

Calm my heart
Lift my soul
Bring me close
Make me whole

Calm my waters
By the stream
Calm my storm
Within my dream

Trust me with you
Be my mate
Calm my waters
Before it's too late

Shield My Love

Shield me protect me
Comfort my soul
Love me forever
Make me your goal

Cushion my body
Shield my heart
Protect my body
Right from the start

Shield my love
Know how I am feeling
Love how I look
Its so appealing

Happy am I
Happy forever
Now you are with me
Please leave me never

Prisoner

The sentence is very clear
As in a court you do appear
The judge passes sentence in his own way
And you are condemned on this very day

Into prison you go unhappily along
Reflecting on your crime and what you did wrong
You are alone confined to a cell
This is your home now this is your hell

With mould and graffiti on the walls all around
Dirty and damp life is profound
For your deathly sentence lasts so long
This is your future it's where you belong

Operation Brainstorm

The brain is a wonderful thing
Full of complexity
What man has achieved is
Written in history

A Norwegian scientist best describes
The working of each part
By explaining to an audience
That it's more complex than the heart

As his experiment did unfold
He clarified the facts
Showing all the working parts
Was a major task

Using simulators to demonstrate a
His three dimensional show
With so many diagram
He was all ready to go

He called his machine brainstorm
It could cure any problems with the brain
This was the ultimate break though
For everyone was now sane

But someone stole his machine
In its only form
So in order to get it back
In came operation brainstorm

The Inner Truth

Exist in the euphoria
Open of all thoughts
In pleasure and splendour
As you have been taught

Maintain your existence
With clarity and truth
Obtain all knowledge
While you are in your youth

Make knowledge your goal
But do not cloud your mind
Proving yourself loving
Trust worthy and kind

Feel your inner thoughts
Share your knowledge of life
And spread the word
For its love that you must strife

Be humble law abiding
Always loyal and true
Give all your love
It's a commitment to you
Fear not the rich man
But think of the poor
The selfish will suffer
The humble will endure

Be honest with yourself
Express all your desires
And you will discover happiness
Before your life expires

So think of this inner truth
That is with you from the start
It travels with you always
Even to the stars

Loves Hope

How clear I see you near to me
As clear as the stars above
But still I fail to understand
What is this thing called love

How fine it is like grains of sand
Or the depths you need to swim
But like shallow thoughts in an empty mind
You fear your losing him
Like a lonely fool
Or an empty pool
And lose him you will
And far from happy
Sad you will be who tastes the bitter pill

Your aching heart does yearn for him
You feel the hurtful pain
Of a lost love and never will remain

Emily In Ecstacy Once More

Thoughts that capture
A restful mind
An imagination of
A different kind

New thoughts dwell
Like a boat on a stream of time
And you travel on it
Like an endless rhyme

Thinking of the things
You love to say
And relaxing so peacefully
At the end of the day

Like a robin in winter
Finding a place to rest
To a place of solitude
Where you make your nest

You prepare yourself
For each season to start
Being adaptable with a
Warmth in your heart

But who is this woman?
A woman of complexity
I reply this is Emily
And she lives in ecstasy

Is ecstasy a place people ask
Trying to be kind
I say it's the best place
It's a place within your mind

Sometimes she seems vacant
Without reason or choice
But although she lives in ecstasy
She still has a voice

Watch the sky above
And let the birds fly free
Let them fly away
And join Emily in ecstasy

Then Came The Rain

My sunny day ended
With the presence of a cloud
Lightning flashed across the sky
And the thunder sounded loud

Thunder was a voice
Lightning was my pain
The sun was my happiness
Then came the rain

Flowers make me happy
Until the fading of the day
Then came the rain
And washed them all away

Once I loved a girl
A love I can't explain
Then came the heartbreak
Then came the rain

The road was so flooded
The water was so deep
Like never ending tear drops
From a person who couldn't weep

So empty is my heart
Confusion in my brain
Once I was so happy
Then came the rain

Ancient Ruins

The sacred place for those that mourn their dead,
It concerns the fortress where lost souls do tread.
On the earth that speaks to you of ancient times,
where soldiers committed their crimes.

The faith of god knows no bounds
And the angels with their spirits surrounds.
A journey through time if you dare to see,
that age was a place and time to be.

Searching souls for answers of the lives once led
For the dead who put their dreams to bed
Where disease and poverty prevailed
And a hero coming from battle was hailed

You now feel the chill that lies in the air
That coldness is like nothing to compare
But the ghost of those left behind
Faint whispers of someone confined

Trapped upon this earth in the ruins of this place
You cannot see his image, you cannot see his face
You just feel his presence as he passes you by
With a whispering voice he never wanted to die
A maiden is also singing and dancing around
Singing so softly its you that she has found

Let The Candles Burn

Let the candles burn through the night
Let it burn now ever so bright
Let it flicker away but never ever go out
May it remind me to never live without a doubt

Let the candles burn and remind me of the truth
Of you and me when we were in our youth
Light up all the room with candles for each year
And may we think of a time when we would shed no tear

While the candle burn I will have company
Light those candles so I can see
Burn away in my room tonight
And forever make it bright

Burning softly in the breeze
Flickering candles putting me at ease
Slowly they go out one by one
Now I know that we are one

The candles were my burning life
Now they are gone I shall take flight
So let the candles burn in heaven instead
And put my thoughts and dreams to bed

The Stone Bridge
By The Stream

As I walk over the old stone bridge over a stream
My heart aches and my eyes gleam
I see you watching me from close by
And realise you wanted to die

We walked hand in hand across that bridge
And into the woods so deep
And now I walk across that bridge
And think of you I begin to weep

Your ghost waits for me each day
And I can only stand there and pray
Pray I would be with you just like before
Holding your hand just like before

The sun rises as you stand waiting for me
On the old stone bridge by the wood
I feel lonely and my heart aches
I would join you if I could

But life is cruel and impossible for me
One day I will join you one day when I am free

Soldier

Here the war cries of many men
Going to war and back again
So proud of his uniform
His stripes and his colours
Shining black boots just like the others

Soldier protects all those of his kind
To live so securely for peace of mind
Patrolling the jungle patrolling the land
Protecting the child take hold of her hand

The army does not discriminate colour or kind
Female soldiers can have peace of mind
The female soldier stands proud as one of the team
They reign over all they are supreme

The soldier is proud and humble too
They fight with courage just to get through
A soldier is trained to survive everywhere
But they learn about compassion and how to care

Nothing is Real

In a world of imagination stood a man with frustration
A man that thought he was real you see
From a game was so unreal to me
He tried to make his way through life
He even invented a wife
And a fantasy woman as well
His life was a living hell
He couldn't even feel
He must have known nothing was real
The warnings were there before his eyes
So listen and ignore their lies
It's written on walls and in the sand
So you know just where you stand
You need to know what is exact
Nothing is real and that is a fact

All or Nothing

Put into life what you have got
Add in some more if you have a lot
Conjure ideas again and again
Keep on going tax your brain

Giving it your effort all your best
Put everything in and sod the rest
Give it your blood give it your soul
Give everything empty your bowl

Make all the effort to be a success
Don't hold nothing back or get in a mess
Follow your fortune follow your fame
Always remember be ahead of the game

Your talent is wasted while you are asleep
So use your time wisely life is not cheap
Be part of the stream flowing smoothly along
Be patient with yourself you can't go wrong

Its all or nothing people will say
That's what I tell stay with it I pray
You will make it in your own way
That's what I will always say
All or nothing

The Vision

Am I hallucinating my minds confused
Did I take something I am so amused
Confused by my thoughts you see
About things that are meant to be

See and hearing strange things by day
Confused by voice what did they say
Dreaming strange dreams at night
Struggling through mud in a fight

Demons are with me I swear
Tossing me up in mid air
Battling spirits in a fire
While living my only desire

Fading in images of my past
Visions pass my eyes so fast
Like the fast motion of a bus or a train
Something's got hold of my brain
How can I tell you how do I explain
It's very likely I am going insane

Time

Time ticks like a clock on the wall
Time passes for you to recall
Forward it goes through the hours of the day
While the children in the schoolyard do play

Ticking away like the sound of a grandfather clock
Each hour chime sounds and the pendulum does rock
Time is your enemy time is your friend
Where did time go when you meet your end

Sea Waves

The waves roll along a beach
Sparking under the sun
By the morn I see
That the day has just begun

Gently it flows across the sand
As clear as can be
With a faint whisper of a sound
All for us to see

So peaceful and flowing
It glides over the sand
Like the beat of my heart
Or the wave of my hand

Away from the chaos
The noise on the street
With the sea waves
Around my bare feet

Sea waves on the ocean
Sea waves on the sand
Moving to music and
The wave of my hand

The Journey

Hustle bustle everywhere
People travel without a care
On buses and trains they have to go
On trams they travel too and fro

In crowded stations all day long
Delays in transport when things go wrong
All hunched up like peas in a pan
Filling the transport wherever they can

Sweaty bodies stand and sit
With bags and cases they try to fit
Chatting some cursing wildly
Suffocating in such misery

Rude people push their way in a queue
With no manners except for a few
With the sound of children screaming so loud
Please rescue me get me out of this crowd

Scotland

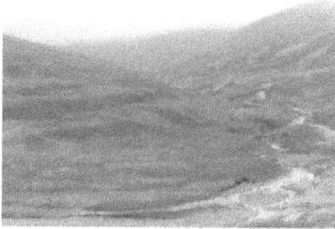

SCOTLAND

Through mountains and glen whispering sound
The highlands of Scotland with views all around
Whispering Gaelic the language of some
The sound of a bagpipe or the sound of a drum

The castles are many as plain as can be
Those mountains are calling come on to me
The stream of clear water flow through valleys so wide
Scotland's own beauty a place full of pride

Your winters are harsh your summers so grand
The sight of the heather grow wild in this land
The wind that blows southward can make a man freeze
And all of that walking brings you to your knees

With whiskey inside you warming your heart
And the love of dear Scotland with you from the start
Give me your haggis give me short bread
But no more whiskey because it's gone to my head

My Best Friend

IN MEMORY OF RICHARD HOWARTH

In times of need
You came to me
A friend of mine
You will ever be

In school days
We worked and played
We lived our lives
And never strayed

Listening to music
Of the day
Sharing experiences
In our own special way

We grew up
And lived our own lives
Both moved away
And married our wives
We both had children
Our own family home
Giving up freedom
Nowhere to roam

In time we reconnected
Together again
Years have passed by us
But were still the same

Supporting each other
By text or by phone
Just letter us know
That were not alone

About The Author

I am Stephen Robert Sutton a writer of novels, artist and writer of poems, I have been writing poems since 1987 and accumulated hundreds of them since this time. I was born in Birmingham and raised in Lichfield in Staffordshire, I moved to Manchester in my early thirties and settled there. The earlier part of my education was at Chadsmead infant and junior school and at Netherstowe comprehensive school, I am dyslexic and dyspraxic which was unheard of at that time in the sixties and early seventies. I educated myself using comics such as the Dandy and the Beano, I later read the American Mad comics, which were easier to understand. Due to not getting the grades at school and college I went back to education in my late thirties and obtained a diploma in welfare studies and other subjects and went on to the university of Salford and graduated as a qualified nurse. It was all about self directed study which I had done as a child, I could deal with that without any problem, although I was assessed by a educational psychologist for dyslexia. At last someone recognised my disability and acted accordingly I did get support by the equality and diversity office at university.

When I started work in the early seventies I had not got a clue what to do, I was in and out of jobs which was easy then due to the amount of jobs around. Eventually I settled down at twenty one as a care assistant in a residential home called Nearfield house in Lichfield I was there for thirteen years until I moved to Pontins in Blackpool and then to Ashton Under Lyne in greater Manchester. I have mentioned my education in Manchester and becoming a nurse which I still am now, I am almost retired and hope to pursue my writing which means more novels and more poetry. The last poem is in memory of a my best friend Richard Howarth who recently past away, November 2019.

Lightning Source UK Ltd.
Milton Keynes UK
UKHW012326120220
358617UK00001B/24